CPER

D0560782

Dear Parents,

Is your child a new reader? If yes, one good way to help your child build confidence and word recognition skills is by introducing word families.

The die-cuts at the bottoms of the pages draw attention to three different word families (letters show through each die-cut shape).

Once your child can read "**ot**", then he or she can focus on the beginning letters and sounds:

> h**ot**, p**ot**, t**ot**

After the single words are learned, the pictures help your child read the words in phrases:

> **hot pot**   **hot tot**
> **snot pot**   **pot on tot**

It's much easier to learn a group of words than to memorize them by sight one word at a time. A sight vocabulary is limited by the number of words that can be held in memory.

Recognizing words by families hugely increases the number of words that your child can know. It gives your child a way to sound out new words (reading specialists call these "word attack" skills), thereby increasing the likelihood he or she will feel successful.

Help your child with the 25 new words in this book by giving him or her multiple chances to read it until all the words are mastered.

Most important, have fun together!

Harriet Ziefert, M.A.
Language Arts/Reading Specialist

Crab Cab

by **Harriet Ziefert**

Illustrated by **Yukiko Kido**

flip-a

WORD

Word Families

The world is full of print. Written words are everywhere. It's impossible to learn printed words by memorizing them word, by word, by word. To make learning easier, words can be grouped into families.

The words in a word family have two or more letters that are the same. We read "ot" words and "ab" words, "it" words and "at" words. If you know "ab," then it's easier to learn cab, dab, and crab.

This book has words from three different word families. All the words in a family rhyme—which means you can add other words to the group by changing the first letter.

It's okay if some of the words you think of are not *real* words. If you make "hab" or "vab" or "zab," it's not wrong— as long as you know the difference between a real word and a nonsense word.

Flip each page and presto-change-o— a new word appears!

The

ot

Family

c
n
k
m
g
p
h
r
d
s
w

snot

†

p o t

hot pot

snot pot

hot tot

pot on tot

The
ab
Family

f
l
w
m
g
n
b
r
d
w
t

crab

b l

d

c a b

crab in a cab

dab on crab

blab in a cab

dab on a cab

The
it
Family

f
l
w
m
g
n
b
r
d
w
t

mitt

h

k n

sit

knit a mitt

sit and knit

hit mitt

sit on mitt

The ot Family

got	hot
lot	pot
snot	tot

The ab Family

blab	cab
crab	dab
grab	scab

The it Family

bit	hit
knit	mitt
sit	spit

Find the words in each family.

Hit snot tot cab hit mitt got grab knit crab sit pot spot mitt hot blab got lot hit tot bit got lot snot hot sit dab spit pot snot pot dab tot scab lot bit grab knit pot dab cab blab bit

Word Family Activities

- Choose two words from the word family and make your own "flip-a-word" illustrations. Remember to make a cut-out at the bottom of the page where the word family shows through.

- Words in a word family rhyme. Learn a song or a poem that rhymes and share it. Or read a book that rhymes and guess which words rhyme.

- Write or tell or draw a story using two or three of the characters in this book. What happens next?